FOOTSTEPS TO FREEDOM
THE UNDERGROUND RAILROAD

GOING UNDERGROUND

AMIE JANE LEAVITT

Peachtree

PURPLE TOAD
PUBLISHING

FOOTSTEPS TO FREEDOM
THE UNDERGROUND RAILROAD

FAMOUS FIGHTERS by Wayne L. Wilson
FREE AT LAST? by Claire O'Neal
GOING UNDERGROUND by Amie Jane Leavitt
THE NEED FOR FLIGHT by Claire O'Neal

Copyright © 2016 by Purple Toad Publishing, Inc.

PUBLISHER'S NOTE

The *Footsteps to Freedom: The Underground Railroad* series covers slavery and racism in United States history. Some of the events told in this series may be disturbing to young readers. The data in this book has been researched in depth, and to the best of our knowledge is factual. Although every measure is taken to give an accurate account, Purple Toad Publishing makes no warranty of the accuracy of the information and is not liable for damages caused by inaccuracies.

ABOUT THE AUTHOR

Amie Jane Leavitt is an accomplished author, researcher, and photographer. She graduated from Brigham Young University as an education major and has since taught all subjects and grade levels in both private and public schools. She is an adventurer who loves to travel the globe in search of interesting story ideas and beautiful places to capture in photos. She has written more than sixty books for kids, has contributed to online and print media, and has worked as a consultant, writer, and editor for numerous educational publishing and assessment companies. Amie has a deep love for American history and for that reason she particularly enjoyed researching and writing this book, *Going Underground*. For her research, she was also able to visit some of the historical sites of the U.G.R.R. and see for herself the hiding places and listen to the stories of the escapes to freedom. To check out a listing of Amie's current projects and published works, visit her website at www.amiejaneleavitt.com.

Printing   1   2   3   4   5   6   7   8   9

Publisher's Cataloging-in-Publication Data

Leavitt, Amie Jane.
  Going Underground / written by Amie Jane Leavitt.
    p. cm.
Includes bibliographic references and index.
ISBN 9781624692192
1. Underground Railroad—Juvenile literature. 2. Antislavery movements—United States—Juvenile literature. I. Series: Footsteps to Freedom The Underground Railroad.
 E450 2016
 973.7115
Library of Congress Control Number: 2015941833   ebook ISBN: 9781624692208

CONTENTS

CHAPTER 1

A Daring Escape

Henry Brown had been born a slave in Richmond, Virginia, in 1816. His owners, John Barret and later William Barret, had never treated him extremely horribly. They had never been whipped him. He had been, for the most part, well fed. And he had always been properly clothed. This was much better than most slaves on other plantations had it, and he knew it.

Yet he was still a slave. Someone else owned him. His breath, his body, and his labor were the property of another man. How could anyone truly be happy in such a situation? Henry wasn't.

One of the things that slaves feared the most was the auction block, where they could be sold like cattle. When they were sold, they were shipped to a master on another plantation. Many of them never saw or heard from friends or family members again.

Henry Box Brown went on to have a career in show business after he escaped to slavery. He performed throughout the North and in Europe.

The Louisiana plantation house where Henry Box Brown was born

Henry wasn't sold at auction, but his wife and children were. He knew they were completely out of his life and he'd never see them again. A piece of him died the day the slave trader carted them away. Henry's heart was broken.

Henry knew he couldn't be a slave for one more minute. He decided that his future would never again be dictated by a master, an overseer, or anyone else. He had to escape—or he would die trying.

Henry was wise enough to know that he could not simply run. Slaves who were caught were often beaten, sold, or even hanged. Every slave knew that you didn't want to get "sold down the river," shipped down the Ohio or Mississippi to an owner in the Deep South. Life on the cotton plantations in the Deep South was brutal.

After giving it a lot of careful thought, Henry came up with a plan. It was risky, and he would have to ask other people for help.

Henry had a friend in town, a free black man named James C.A. Smith. James contacted Samuel A. Smith, a white merchant who wanted to help the slaves. Henry told Samuel his plan and asked if he would help. Samuel agreed.

Samuel knew that he was putting himself in danger. If a free person was caught helping slaves escape, he or she could be fined or placed in prison, or both. But Samuel was willing to take the risk.

The plan was this: Brown and the Smiths would work together to build a wooden box that was approximately 3 feet deep, 2 feet wide, and 3 feet long. Once the box was finished, Henry would climb inside. Then Samuel would nail the lid on top and paint in bold letters the address for Philadelphia's Anti-Slavery Office. Samuel would contact the office ahead of time and alert the agents that there was a special "package" being sent to them, and they should open it immediately upon arrival.

The box containing Brown was received by William Still. He said, "The witnesses will never forget that moment. Saw and hatchet quickly had the lid off, and the marvelous resurrection of Brown ensued."

On the day that Henry was to be shipped, the men said their farewells. Then Henry climbed inside the box. The only thing he carried was a small container of water and a few biscuits for the journey. Once Henry had crouched inside, Samuel carefully nailed it closed and sent the box on its way. Samuel was likely nervous that day as he watched the wagon carting Henry away inside a box.

Henry's voyage to freedom was grueling. He spent 27 hours in transport across 350 miles. Along the way, he was tossed to and fro on the back of wagons, thrown onto train platforms, and then hauled across the bumpy streets of Philadelphia. Sometimes the box was tipped upside-down, and Henry had to rest on his head. He was not a small man, either. He weighed 200 pounds and stood at 5 feet 10 inches tall.

Being cramped inside a small box must have been incredibly painful at times. Yet Henry knew all this agony would be worth it if he could just make it to Philadelphia—his first stop on the road to freedom.

Just as Samuel probably felt concern for Henry, so did the people at the Anti-Slavery office. They knew that a package was arriving in the mail and that it contained a human being. Would the man inside survive the journey?

As soon as the box arrived at the antislavery office on March 24, 1849, the agents tore the lid off the crate. They were very pleased with what they found. Henry was hot, sweaty, and a little bruised—but he was alive!

When the last plank was removed, Henry crawled out of the box and stretched his back, legs, and arms. Then, with a big smile, he reportedly shook the hands of everyone in the room and said, "How do you do, gentlemen?"[1] Then he sang a prayer of thanksgiving, based on the Bible's Psalm 40:

I waited patiently for the Lord;
and he inclined unto me, and heard my cry.
He brought me up also out of a horrible pit, out of the miry clay,
and set my feet upon a rock, and established my goings.
And he hath put a new song in my mouth,
even praise unto our God:
many shall see it, and fear, and shall trust in the Lord.[2]

A few weeks after they shipped Henry, the Smiths tried to mail more slaves from Richmond to Philadelphia. They were both arrested. James was not convicted, but Samuel was. He was sentenced to six and a half years in jail.

The escape of Henry Box Brown—as he would be known from then on—became one of the most famous escapes in all of Underground Railroad history. It showed what extreme lengths people were willing to go to in order to remove themselves from the shackles of slavery. It also showed that successful escape stories often required the help of many others along the way. Henry would not have been able to ship himself to Philadelphia without the aid of James and Samuel Smith. And if there hadn't been someone to receive and open the package, Henry would have been doomed.

It took the help of many people to ensure the freedom of runaway slaves. And that network of people, all working together for a common good, was known as the Underground Railroad.

Fear in the North

It took a great amount of courage to get involved with the Underground Railroad. Laws like the Fugitive Slave Act of 1850 made it illegal to help a runaway slave. If a slave was found in the North, he or she was to be handed over to the authorities. If a person in the North did not comply with this law, they could be fined $1,000 and imprisoned for six months. This fine was particularly steep. In today's money, that $1,000 would be similar to $30,000!

Many runaway slaves that made it to the North were later captured and taken back to their lives of bondage.

A hero is someone who helps someone else without thinking of the consequences to himself or herself. The people who served in any capacity on the Underground Railroad and with abolitionism in general were true heroes. They helped for many reasons. They helped because it was the right thing to do. Some helped because their religious convictions and their innermost soul told them that slavery was wrong. They helped because they too had been slaves and they wanted to help others to freedom.

We do not know the names of many of the helpers on the Underground Railroad. However, some of the most famous helpers and supporters of the Underground Railroad were Harriet Tubman, Levi Coffin, William Still, Frederick Douglass, Thomas Garrett, William Lloyd Garrison, John Brown, Samuel Green, Gerrit Smith, and Lucretia Mott.

CHAPTER 2

A Secret Network

Sometimes, when people hear the term *Underground Railroad,* they imagine a train that zips through tunnels below the surface of the earth, taking both railcars and passengers on a journey through inky darkness. However, that imagery is not what the term *Underground Railroad* is referring to. The word *underground* in this case means "secret" or "concealed." The word *railroad* refers to a specific "network" or "system." The Underground Railroad was a secret network of people who helped slaves escape to freedom.

It is believed that the first informal efforts to aid slaves in their flight for freedom occurred in the late 1600s. However, these efforts were not called the Underground Railroad back then, because trains and the railroad had not even been invented yet! The high point of the Underground Railroad—the time when the lines carried the most traffic—was just before the Civil War, from the 1830s to the 1860s.

This statue, located in Detroit, Michigan, shows a group of runaway slaves with their "conductor," who is showing them the way to Canada.

Without the help of an Underground Railroad, Robert Brown risked crossing the Potomac on horseback alone on Christmas night in 1865 to escape his captors.

No one knows for certain where the term *Underground Railroad* came from, although there are some legends about its origins. The most common one dates from 1831. The story goes that a slave owner from Kentucky was in hot pursuit of his runaway slave named Tice Davids. The slave owner had nearly caught Davids near the Ohio River, but when he reached the town of Ripley, Ohio, Davids had disappeared. It was as if he had been swallowed by the earth. Frustrated, the slave owner said that Davids disappeared as if "he had gone off on an underground railroad!" The slave owner did not realize how accurate his description was. Many other slaves had made their way through Ripley at that time, hidden by people in the community who belonged to a "secret network." When the slave owner had given up his search, the runaway was shuttled to another location farther north.[1]

The people who helped runaway slaves during this time came from many walks of life. Some were former slaves who had escaped to freedom, had purchased their freedom, or had been granted their freedom by former masters. Some were northern blacks who had been born free. Some were members of particular religious groups, such as the Quakers, who were against the institution of slavery. Some were abolitionists, people who fought openly to abolish or do away with the practice. Some were members of Native American tribes who gave the runaway slaves shelter and invited them to become part of their communities.[2]

Slave catchers would send bloodhounds and other dogs after runaway slaves.

Being part of the Underground Railroad, or U.G.R.R., was dangerous for everyone involved. For the runaways, serious beatings or even death could be the result if caught. They were hunted like animals, with bloodhounds tracking them through forests, swamps, and fields.

U.G.R.R. agents were also in grave danger. There were laws in the United States that protected the rights of property owners. And slaves were considered property, just as a wagon, chair, plow, or farm animal was. People who helped this "property" escape were breaking the law and could be sent to prison or charged hefty fines. The U.G.R.R. agents were also in danger from brutal slave hunters who did not care who got hurt as they chased their bounty.

The people involved in the U.G.R.R. knew it was crucial to keep quiet. Most people did not talk about their activities at all. Others used secret codes when

Code Word	Meaning
agent	a person who coordinates escapes for slaves
conductor	a person who guides or escorts slaves to safety
brakeman	a person who helps runaway slaves find homes and jobs when they reach freedom
forward	to send slaves from one station to another
freedom train, gospel train	the Underground Railroad
friend with friends	a conductor escorting runaways
heaven, Promised Land	Canada
lost a passenger	a runaway has been caught
passenger	a runaway on the Underground Railroad
station	a safe place (house, barn, business, church, etc.) where runaways were hidden and sheltered
stationmaster	a person who provides shelter for runaways at his or her station
stockholder	a person who provides money, transportation, or goods to support runaways
the wind blows from the South today	runaway slaves are in the area

they spoke or wrote to one another. These codes often included common railroad terms to disguise the real activities of the Underground Railroad.

For example, a real train carries passengers, cargo, boxes, packages, and baggage. On the Underground Railroad, these words described runaway slaves. A person who takes care of passengers on a train is called a conductor. On the Underground Railroad, a person who took runaway slaves from place to place or guided them to freedom was called a conductor. Trains generally make stops at safe locations called stations. On the Underground Railroad, a safe place that a runaway slave would stop—such as a business, home, barn, or church—was called either a "stop" or a "station." On busy routes, stations were usually about 12 to 15 miles apart—the distance an average person could travel in one night's journey. The person who owned this station—the business owner, homeowner, or clergy

member—would be a called a stationmaster. In a traditional railroad or other business, people can buy shares or stocks. The money is used to help the business grow, and in return, these stockholders own a small part of the business. On the Underground Railroad, stockholders were people who gave money, goods, or transportation to help runaways on their journey. Agents or operatives on a train help organize schedules and shipments. So, too, did the agents and operatives on the Underground Railroad. Their job was to help make the transition from place to place more organized and therefore more successful.

In 1857, a man named G. S. Nelson from Reading, Pennsylvania,

John W. Jones was born into slavery, but escaped. He and a small group of runaway slaves traveled 300 miles to New York.

wrote two letters to William Still, an abolitionist and civil rights activist in Philadelphia. In these letters, Nelson talks in secret code using words like "packages" and "goods" to describe the runaway slaves—two children and two adults—whom he is hiding in his home. These letters were later published in Still's book *The Underground Railroad*. Notice how worried Nelson is that the "packages" remain safe. He knows that there are people in the area (slave hunters) who are searching for them and wants to do everything he can to keep them out of harm's way:

Mr. Still—My Dear Sir—I suppose you are somewhat uneasy because the goods did not come safe to hand on Monday evening, as you expected— consigned from Harrisburg to you. The train only was from Harrisburg to

William Still

Reading, and as it happened, the goods had to stay all night with us, and as some excitement exists here about goods of the kind, we thought it expedient and wise to detain them until we could hear from you. There are two small boxes and two large ones; we have them all secure; what had better be done? Let us know. Also, as we can learn, there are three more boxes still in Harrisburg. Answer your communication at Harrisburg. Also, fail not to answer this by the return of mail, as things are rather critical, and you will oblige us.

G. S. Nelson[3]

Another way that people helped on the Underground Railroad was by making clothing for the fugitives. Tattered and torn clothing clearly marked people as escapees. Women in the North would organize Anti-Slavery Sewing Societies, where they would work together hour upon hour, sewing clothing for the slaves who would travel through their area. This act of service was crucial. With a decent shirt and pair of pants for men and a homespun dress for women, the escapees could blend in more easily in the North.

There were anti-slavery committees all across the North. This picture from 1851 shows one in Pennsylvania with Lucretia Mott (second from right in the front row) as a member.

The Records of William Still

William Still, known as the Father of the Underground Railroad, was one of the main U.G.R.R. leaders in Philadelphia. It is estimated that he helped more than 800 slaves escape to freedom on the eastern line of the U.G.R.R.

Most people involved in the U.G.R.R. did not keep written records—it was too dangerous. William Still, however, did keep records. He believed these documents could help reunite families that had been torn apart by slavery.[4]

Over his 14 years in the U.G.R.R., he wrote a description of every person who came through his station. He kept letters that he received in the mail and made handwritten copies of those he sent. He was careful with his records, storing them inside a crypt at the local cemetery. The documents stayed safe there all the way through the Civil War.

In the 1870s, Still published his recollections, notes, and correspondence in a book called *The Underground Railroad*.[5] It is considered one of the best remaining sources on the activities of the U.G.R.R. Many of his associates, including William Lloyd Garrison and other abolitionists, endorsed the book. They felt that Still had done a great job of capturing what life and work on the U.G.R.R. was really like.[6]

Just as Still had hoped, *The Underground Railroad* helped many families find their loved ones. Even today, people can use this book to find out about their slave ancestors and their brave escape to freedom.

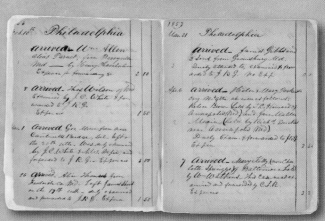

Still's journal recorded arriving slaves

CHAPTER 3

Riding the Rails

Many slave owners in the South tried to paint a false picture of slavery. They wanted people in the North to believe that people actually enjoyed being slaves and were grateful to their masters for providing them with work, clothing, homes, and food. They spread the message that black people were inferior to whites, and they could not possibly survive on their own. Perhaps telling stories like these made the slave owners feel justified about keeping more than 4 million people in bondage.

The proof against these stories was abundant. Daily, slaves tried to escape, risking their lives to do so. They wanted freedom.

In a story that is similar to Henry Box Brown's, 25-year-old William Gilliam wanted his freedom. A slave since birth, he ran from his widowed owner in Richmond, Virginia, to Canada via the eastern line of the Underground Railroad. Shortly after he arrived in the Promised Land, as Canada was called, he received a letter from her. (It

People in the South tried to compare slavery to the factory system in industrialized areas. This cartoon from 1861 shows dancing slaves in America compared to downtrodden factory workers in England.

had been forwarded by a common associate.) In her letter, the woman tried to make Gilliam feel guilty for leaving. She wanted him to feel sorry for her! She said that because he wasn't around anymore to be hired out to make a living for her, she was in the poor house with very little to eat. Gilliam never responded to the lady, but he did discuss the matter with his friend in another letter. He wrote, "I have no compassion on the penniless widow lady. I have served her 25 years and 2 months, I think that is long enough for me to live [as] a slave." He signed his letter, "William Gilliam, the Widow's Mite," which is a reference to a story in the Bible that means he has given her all he can give.[1]

Many people left slave life as a matter of survival. They were physically abused by their masters and overseers. They were often whipped until their backs had layers of deep scars. They were forced to work long hours—sometimes from dawn to dusk. They were given very little. They had inadequate housing: many lived in small shacks with only dirt for a floor. For some, the physical abuse was so severe

Slaves were sometimes forced to whip their fellow slaves.

Slaves were truly treated like animals—or worse. This gruesome slave collar was meant to prevent slaves from escaping.

that they knew they would die from the mistreatment. Many of these people felt they had nothing to lose by trying to escape to freedom. If they made it, they would have a much better life. If they did not make it and died trying, then they were really no worse off than they had been in bondage.

Some runaway slaves came up with very specific escape plans, as Henry Box Brown had. The plans were ingenious and creative. Some dressed in disguises: men dressed as women, women dressed as men, and some made themselves appear white by putting a special powder on their bodies. Others put on grand theatrical productions to throw off slave hunters. One group pretended that they were going to a funeral and wept and wailed as they traveled along in their wagon. Most slaves would agree that it was better to have a plan. Just taking off randomly and running out into the forest without a clear direction usually led to disaster.

Some slaves escaped by land. Others escaped by boat.

Most slaves traveled on foot, running as much as they could. Others used a combination of transportation. Some hid in steam trunks. Some hid in secret boxes on the beds of wagons. Some traveled on horseback or on trains.

Some slaves were lucky enough to know people they could trust and who were willing to help them. Oftentimes, these trusted individuals knew people who worked in the Underground Railroad. Jane, a slave in Kentucky, found out that she and her daughter were being sold down the river. She immediately asked a sympathetic neighbor couple to help her. They contacted a friend in Cincinnati, Ohio, who was part of the Underground Railroad. This man agreed to help. Jane was to slip out of the house at night with her daughter. The neighbor would take them to the river dock, where they would meet the conductor, who would row them across the Ohio River. All of this had to be carefully orchestrated: one slip-up and the whole plan could be ruined. Jane had to make sure she and her child were not detected when they left the house. Then she had to make it to the river dock without being spotted. Finally, her conductor needed to get her safely across the river and into a hiding place. Fortunately for Jane, the plan worked. Once she and her daughter arrived in the North, they spent two weeks at the home of stationmasters Levi and Catharine Coffin before continuing on to Canada.[2]

Not all slaves had a network of people they could count on. They may have heard of the Underground Railroad but had no idea how to get a "ticket" to ride it. Slaves in this situation just left on their own and hoped for the best. They slipped into the woods or journeyed into marshy swamps and bogs. They hid in barns and thickets and other out-of-the-way places. Sometimes they were lucky and a kind person would give them food and shelter and direct them to other people who were likeminded. However, sometimes they met people who did not agree with slave escapes and turned the law on them.

Some slaves were fortunate enough to have a conductor to either give them tips along the way or guide them throughout their journey. Harriet Tubman was one of the most famous conductors on the Underground Railroad. She had grown up as a slave and had escaped to freedom when she was 30 years old. She fled with her brothers and used the North Star to guide her travels. She made it safely to freedom—but she wasn't satisfied to have only her own sovereignty. She wanted to help others obtain freedom too.

Repeatedly risking her life, Tubman journeyed back into the South nineteen times to help others. She became known as the Moses of her people, because like Moses of the Bible, who guided the Israelites out of bondage in Egypt, she too led her people to freedom. She was so despised and feared by slave owners that at one point, she had a $40,000 bounty on her head.[3] That is about $1.2 million in today's money.[4]

Harriet Tubman was a famous conductor on the Underground Railroad.

Tubman considered her slave rescues to be serious business. She carried a gun for two reasons: to protect the slaves from slave hunters and to serve as a warning to the runaway slaves whom she led. The slaves knew ahead of time that if they committed themselves to going with her, there was no turning back. She would shoot them before she would allow them to return and put the rest of the group in jeopardy. If slaves decided to escape with Harriet Tubman as their guide, it was all or nothing.

Harriet Tubman

Runaway Slave Ads

A runaway slave ad

Whenever slaves left their plantation without their owner, they had to have a pass that said they had permission to be off the owner's property. If slaves were caught without a pass, they were immediately arrested. Because of that, many runaways had fake passes made for them.

When a slave escaped, the owner generally put an ad in the paper offering a reward for the person's capture and return. The reward varied depending upon how valuable the owner felt the slave was. Some slaves were worth only $25 to an owner. Other slaves could be valued at hundreds or thousands of dollars.

In the ad, the owner would state the name of the slave and give a physical description of him or her. The ad would give information about special markings or scars that the person might have, what clothes he or she was wearing at the time of the escape, and the person's age. It would also state from where the slave had run and where he or she might be going. The bottom of the ad included the slave owner's contact information.

Some ads included names and descriptions of several runaways.

CHAPTER 4

Many Routes

Many slaves traveled north on the Underground Railroad. They hid in the daytime and traveled at night, using the North Star to guide them. They did not travel specific routes to get to the north, and many did not have a specific destination in mind—as long as they would be free in the new land. Some traveled up from Kentucky, across the Ohio River, and then into the free states of Ohio and Indiana. Others traveled across the Missouri Territory into Illinois and Michigan. Others left plantations in Virginia and Maryland and traveled north into Pennsylvania and New Jersey and beyond.

The center of the U.G.R.R. was the Ohio River Valley. There were dozens of places along the Ohio River that could be crossed by boat, by swimming, or by walking (in times of drought or when the river was frozen). Once the runaways crossed the river, they could move northward from farm to farm all the way to Canada. It is estimated that 100,000 slaves escaped to freedom

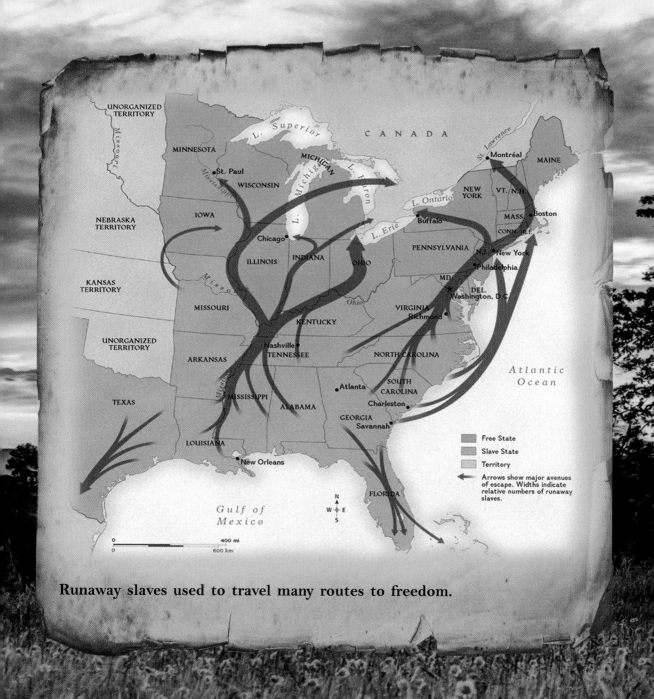

Runaway slaves used to travel many routes to freedom.

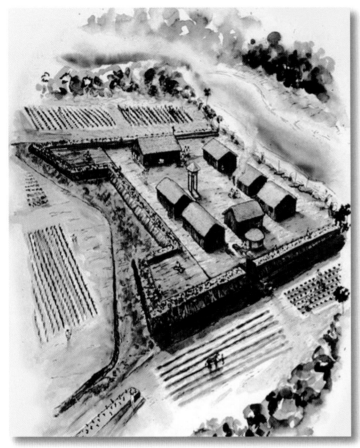

The first free African American community was Fort Mose in St. Augustine, Florida.

along the Underground Railroad, and 40,000 of those passed through the state of Ohio.[1]

Some slaves fled south to the untamed wilderness of Florida. In fact, Spanish-controlled Florida was the main destination for travelers on the first slave-escape network. In the 1600s and 1700s, the Spanish encouraged this exodus and welcomed the fleeing slaves to its territory.

In 1738, years before the Revolutionary War, the Spanish set up the first free black community in North America. Runaway slaves could start new lives there. This community, called Fort Mose[2] (pronounced Mo-ZAY), was located on the Atlantic Coast near present-day St. Augustine.[3]

Some runaway slaves in Florida found refuge with the Seminole Indians. They lived with the Seminoles and sometimes intermarried. Eventually, these people were referred to as Black Seminoles. In treaties with the Seminoles, the U.S. government tried to include requirements that the Indians had to return any runaway slaves they found. The Seminoles rarely followed this rule[4]

Other slaves fled by running southwestward toward Mexico, where slavery had been abolished in 1829.[5] Others moved westward into the territories—regions that were not yet states. Some even hopped ships and traveled across the Atlantic,

settling on the islands of the Caribbean or farther south in the countries of South America.[6]

Levi Coffin was a Quaker, an abolitionist, and an active stationmaster on the Underground Railroad. He was born in North Carolina and for the first part of his married life he and his wife, Catharine, lived in Indiana. Then they moved to Cincinnati, Ohio. In both Indiana and Ohio, the couple opened their home to travelers on the Underground Railroad. It is estimated that during the 20 years they lived in Indiana, around 2,000 slaves passed through their station. That is about 100 slaves per year, a number that earned their busy home the nickname Grand Central Station. In this Indiana home, the couple had a secret room that was accessible from a small door in the bedroom wall. When slaves were hiding there, a bed was placed in front of the door to hide its existence.[7]

Sometimes the slaves would stay at the Coffins' home for several weeks; the couple wanted the runaways to have enough time to regain their strength before they continued on their journey. Coffin would arrange transportation for them both to and from his house. Conductors sometimes took them; other times, Coffin would hide them in his wagon and drive them himself. Because of his immense success in helping runaways in both Indiana and Ohio, he is often called the President of the Underground Railroad.

Traffic on the Underground Railroad was sometimes unpredictable. As Levi Coffin wrote:

We knew not what night or what hour of the night we would be roused from slumber by a gentle rap at the door. That was the signal announcing

Levi Coffin

The attic of Levi Coffin's house was often used to hide runaway slaves.

the arrival of a train of the Underground Railroad, for the locomotive did not whistle, nor make any unnecessary noise. I have often been awakened by this signal, and sprang out of bed in the dark and opened the door. Outside in the cold or rain, there would be a two-horse wagon loaded with fugitives, perhaps the greater part of them women and children."[8]

As the slaves traveled toward their final destinations, they hid the best they could. If they were lucky enough to be

directed to a safe house or station on the U.G.R.R., they might get a warm meal and a place to sleep for a day or two or even several weeks. At these stations, runaway slaves might get to sleep in a hay barn. Or they could be brought into a home and allowed to eat and sleep inside. If a slave hunter came around, then the slaves would be hurried to a hiding place in the house. Some houses had hidden cupboards large enough to hold several people. Some houses had secret staircases. Others had attics with secret doors. The slaves would be stowed in these places only until the slave hunter went on his way.

An indoor well in the Coffin house was another place for runaways to hide.

The Rankin House is a National Historical Landmark. It overlooks the Ohio River and is open for guided tours.

The Reverend John Rankin's home in Ripley, Ohio, was another important station on the Underground Railroad. It stood on a large hill, appropriately named Liberty Hill, that was about 650 feet above the level of the Ohio River. People on the other side of the river (in the slave state of Kentucky) and people who were crossing the river could easily see the house perched on its hill. One story says that Rankin would hang a lantern inside his window as a sign that his home was a safe place for runaway slaves to stop. Another story says that the lantern was hung outside on a tall pole. Sometimes as many as 12 runaways were in Rankin's home at one time. When slave hunters came prowling, he would hide the slaves in a cubbyhole in the attic or down in the cellar.[9]

Rankin wasn't afraid of confronting slave hunters when they came to his house. Often, he had a gun in his hand and his adult sons at his side for protection.[10] In 1835, Rankin helped start the Ohio chapter of the Anti-Slavery Society. He established the Free Presbyterian Church of America, which he refused to allow slave owners to join. Years later, when Harriet Beecher Stowe wrote her famous

Thomas Garrett

book *Uncle Tom's Cabin,* she included John Rankin's home as the first stop that one of the main characters (Eliza) made in Ohio.[11]

Quaker and abolitionist Thomas Garrett was a prominent stationmaster on the eastern line of the Underground Railroad. He lived in Chester County, Pennsylvania, and he often had contact with another famous stationmaster, William Still of Philadelphia. He had been involved in the Underground Railroad ever since he was a child—his family often hid runaway slaves in their farmhouse in Delaware. During his adult life, he was responsible for assisting nearly 2,700 slaves on their journey to freedom.[12] In the late 1840s, he was tried and found guilty of violating the Fugitive Slave Act. The hefty fines cost him all of his money and property. Yet even with this crippling loss, he stood bravely in the courtroom and vowed that he would continue to help runaway slaves whenever he could.

Thornfield was the first home of Thomas Garrett. It is located in Pennsylvania and remains a private residence.

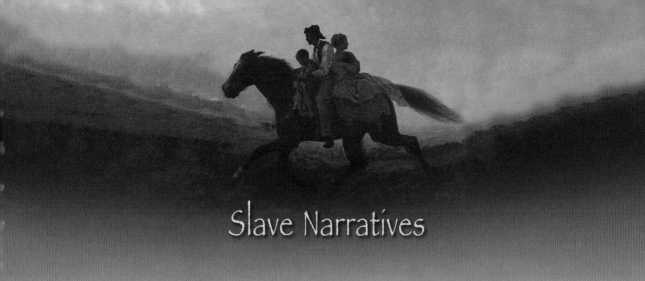

Slave Narratives

Most slaves were not taught how to read and write. So, unfortunately, many of the slave narratives that we have today were not written in the hand of the slaves themselves. However, Frederick Douglass was a well-educated former slave. His book, *Life and Times of Frederick Douglass,* is a true autobiographical account. The title page states that fact clearly: it was "Written by Himself."

In this book, Douglass describes his childhood in slavery. He tells how he escaped from bondage. He tells how he got involved in the anti-slavery movement. He describes the work that he did in the United States and in Great Britain as an abolitionist. He includes information about how he published his newspaper, *The North Star,* from 1847 to 1851. He tells of his specific work with the Underground Railroad. He also includes some of the interviews and conversations he had with his friend, President Abraham Lincoln.

One of the great advantages of the Internet is the availability of free resources. This book, in its entirety is available online.

Title page of *Life and Times of Frederick Douglass*

CHAPTER 5

Touring the U.G.R.R.

Many of the places on the Underground Railroad are long gone. Some buildings were kept so secret that no one even knew they were part of the network. However, some places have been officially documented as part of the U.G.R.R. and have been preserved. Visitors can see the secret staircases, cupboards, and attics where the slaves hid, and hear the stories of nighttime arrivals of conductors and their precious cargo. Tour guides describe the heated disputes that sometimes occurred between slave hunters and stationmasters. Some historical sites offer colorful reenactments of historical events.

The National Park Service has compiled an online list of nearly 70 sites in 20 states plus the District of Columbia. Some sites were the homes of leading abolitionists, while others were stations on the railroad. Peter Mott's house in New Jersey, John Brown's cabin in Kansas, and the homes of Levi Coffin, John Rankin, and Thomas Garret

34

The Peter Mott House is located in New Jersey. It was a station on the Underground Railroad and is open for guided tours.

Spring Hill

are only a few of places on the list. Each house is slightly different in what it offers. Some are not open to the public, since they are privately owned.

The state of Ohio has the most documented U.G.R.R. sites in the National Park Service registry. There are 13 locations throughout the state, and the Spring Hill house in Massillon is one of them. This home was built in 1821 by Thomas and Charity Rotch (pronounced "roach'), a Quaker couple from New England. While they lived in Ohio, they provided runaway slaves a safe place to stop in their home. The fugitives stayed either in the basement kitchen or in the second-floor living area with the family. A secret staircase led from the basement to the second floor—but it skipped the first floor entirely. Doors on each end concealed it. People could move from the basement to the upstairs, or from the upstairs to the basement, without being noticed on the first floor. A secret area of the attic could also hide people. Charity Rotch sometimes wrote about the U.G.R.R. activities that took place in the house in her journal. She also mentioned their abolitionist activities in letters to her sister, who lived in the East. As far as the records indicate, no slaves were ever caught by slave hunters at Spring Hill, even though slave hunters did come to the house on many occasions.[1]

At the National Underground Railroad Freedom Center in Cincinnati, visitors can see an actual slave pen that was built in 1830 in Kentucky. It was taken apart

An actual slave pen that held slaves before they were sold at auction is on display in Ohio.

and rebuilt at the museum. The slave trader who built the pen used it as a holding place for the slaves whom he planned to sell at auction. The building was two stories high and had eight small barred windows, a fireplace on one end, and down the center a heavy chain with iron rings to shackle the prisoners. One visitor to the museum said that the feeling inside the slave pen was similar to the feeling he felt when he visited the Nazi concentration camps in Europe. It is estimated that the man who built the slave pen made around $50,000 per year selling slaves. That would have been well over a million dollars in today's money.[2]

The museum also plays a film that shows a reenactment of a flight for freedom. In it, two historical figures (John Rankin and John Parker) help a slave woman along the Underground Railroad. By the time visitors leave the museum, they often have a better understanding of the horrors of slavery and the toll it took on the people who lived in it and on the entire country at large.

Detroit, Michigan, was one of the last stops for people on a western line of the Underground Railroad. Once runaway slaves got here, all they had to do was cross the Detroit River and they would be safe in Windsor, Canada. Today, in the downtown area's Hart Plaza, a memorial commemorates Detroit's role in the Underground Railroad. It shows six runaway slaves getting ready to board a boat to Canada. A conductor stands in the center pointing to the other side. This

This monument in Canada celebrates the freedom that slaves found in the north.

conductor is supposed to be George DeBaptiste, who was an important member of Detroit's Underground Railroad.

On the other side of the river in Canada stands another monument. This one has a 22-foot-high tower in the center that represents a candle. At the base of the candle are three statues: a Quaker woman who is welcoming the slaves to Canada's shores, and the same husband and wife from the Detroit memorial. The wife clutches a baby in her arms, and the man raises his hands in celebration as if to say, "I'm free at last!"

Visitors often wonder what happened to the other runaway slaves who are included in the Detroit memorial. One interpretation is that the absence of these people shows the sad truth about the flight to freedom: not everyone made it successfully to the Promised Land. Some were captured by slave hunters and taken back to slavery. Others died along the way from injury, illness, or hunger. The two memorials are collectively called *The International Underground Railroad Memorial.*[3]

In New Bedford, Massachusetts, stands a home that was once owned by a prosperous African-American

couple, Nathan and Polly Johnson. This two-story dwelling was a station on the Underground Railroad, and one of the slaves who stayed there in 1838 was Frederick Douglass. Douglass was a former slave who eventually became one of the most noted abolitionists of the nineteenth century. He became Abraham Lincoln's personal friend and adviser during the Civil War.[4] At age 20, Douglass (who was then known as Frederick Augustus Washington Bailey) decided he was finished with slavery. He disguised himself in a sailor's uniform and then trekked north. From the southern city of Baltimore, Maryland, Douglass took many modes of transportation: he started on a train, then took a ferry, then another train, then a steamboat, and finally a train again. In less than 24 hours, he was in New York City. However, in order to stay safe, he knew he needed to go even farther north. His final stop was at the Johnson home in New Bedford.

Douglass recalled in his book *My Bondage and My Freedom,* published in 1855, "Mr. Johnson assured me that no slaveholder could take a slave from New Bedford; that there were men there who would lay down their lives, before such an outrage could be perpetuated." New Bedford seemed like the ideal place for Douglass to make his

Frederick Douglass was a famous abolitionist and friend of Abraham Lincoln.

The home on the left is where Douglass first found refuge in New Bedford.

home, at least for the next six years. The Johnson house, where Douglass first found refuge in the city, is now the headquarters of the city's Historical Society. It is also a site on the National Underground Railroad Network to Freedom.[5]

Slavery was an outmoded institution that should never have existed in a "free" land. However, even in the darkest of times during the 300-year history of slavery on this continent, the good in human nature was able to shine through. Shining brightly were the efforts of those on the Underground Railroad. Slaves risked everything for the chance at a better life. People who worked on the U.G.R.R. also risked everything—their lives, their fortunes, and their freedom. Yet they willingly did so. They couldn't stand by and not help while fellow human beings suffered. These heroes of the Underground Railroad continue to inspire others to stand up for human rights against racism and other forms of discrimination.

Fact or Fiction: Quilts of the Underground Railroad

There is a lot of debate about the role that quilts played in the Underground Railroad. Some people believe that slaves made quilts and stitched symbols and codes into their patterns as a way for other slaves to know the routes to travel to freedom. When the slaves ran away, they would take these quilts with them and use them as a map.

Many historians do not believe that slaves used quilts in this manner. Slaves had to move quickly, and they would not have been able to lug around a heavy quilt. Also, if the slaves really did sew symbols and routes into quilts, surely the slaveholders would have gotten wise to this and been able to know where to catch their escapees. Besides these practical reasons, historians also argue that they have found no place in written records to prove that quilts were used as maps on the Underground Railroad.[6]

Many people believe quilts like this one contain codes that helped escaping slaves through their journey along the Underground Railroad.

1793   The Fugitive Slave Act of the United States outlaws any efforts to obstruct the capture of runaway slaves.

1817   Frederick Douglass is born into slavery in Maryland.

1826   On a Mississippi River steamer, 77 slaves mutiny and escape to Indiana.

1831   In Boston, William Lloyd Garrison starts his abolitionist newspaper *The Liberator*.

1838   Frederick Douglass escapes from slavery.

1847   In Rochester, New York, Frederick Douglass starts his abolitionist newspaper *North Star*.

1849   Harriet Tubman escapes to Pennsylvania and later returns to the South 19 times to rescue more than 300 people. Henry Box Brown ships himself to Pennsylvania.

1850   A harsher Fugitive Slave Law than the 1793 law is passed. It allows slave catchers and owners to pursue fugitives into free territory.

1851   In Boston, Massachusetts, a black abolitionist crashes into a courtroom to rescue a fugitive.

1852   *Uncle Tom's Cabin,* by Harriet Beecher Stowe, is published.

1854   The Kansas-Nebraska Act allows each state to decide if they will allow slavery.

1857   The Dred Scott Decision is delivered by the U.S. Supreme Court.

1859   Radical abolitionist John Brown raids Harpers Ferry.

1860   Abraham Lincoln becomes the first Republican to win the United States Presidency.

1861   The U.S. Civil War begins.

1863   The Emancipation Proclamation frees the slaves in Rebel territory only.

1865   The Civil War ends. The 13th Amendment to the U.S. Constitution abolishes slavery in all states.

Chapter 1. A Daring Escape

1. *Underground Railroad: The William Still Story*, PBS Video, http://video.pbs.org/video/2181724307/
2. "The Emergence of Henry 'Box' Brown," *University of North Carolina Free Press,* http://uncpress.unc.edu/pdfs/SampleChapters/9780807831960_ernest_narrative_introsec1.pdf

Chapter 2. A Secret Network

1. "Ohio's Underground Railroad to Freedom," *Ohio State Parks Magazine,* http://www.dnr.state.oh.us/parks/magazinehome/magazine/sprsum96/undergrr/tabid/299/default.aspx
2. Bruce Smith, "For a Century, The First Underground Railroad Ran Slaves South to Florida," *The Huffington Post,* March 18, 2012, http://www.huffingtonpost.com/2012/03/18/first-underground-railroad-ran-south_n_1358253.html
3. William Still, *Still's Underground Railroad Records, Revised Edition* (Philadelphia: William Still, Publisher, 1886), pp. 44–45.
4. Ibid., p. xxxii.
5. Still Family Library, Temple University, http://stillfamily.library.temple.edu/historical-perspective/william-still-significance
6. Still, p.xliii.

Chapter 3. Riding the Rails

1. William Still, *Still's Underground Railroad Records, Revised Edition* (Philadelphia: William Still, Publisher, 1886), pp. 54–58.
2. Levi Coffin, *Reminiscences of Levi Coffin, the Reputed President of the Underground Railroad* (Cincinnati: Robert Clarke & Co., 1880), pp. 328–334.
3. Documenting the American South: "Harriet, the Moses of her People," http://docsouth.unc.edu/neh/harriet/harriet.html
4. Measuring Worth: http://www.measuringworth.com/uscompare/

Chapter 4. Many Routes

1. Ohio's Underground Railroad Freedom Stations: Traveling the State's Underground Railroad, DiscoverOhio.com, http://consumer.discoverohio.com/downloads/presskits/blackhistory/OhioUndergroundRailroad_brochure.pdf
2. British Fort, National Park Service, http://www.nps.gov/nr/travel/underground/fl1.htm
3. Fort Mose Historic State Park, Florida State Parks.org, http://www.floridastateparks.org/fortmose/

4. Bob Beatty, "Tracks to Freedom: Central Florida and the Underground Railroad," http://freedomcenter.org/sites/default/files/Reflections%20from%20Central%20Flordia%20by%20Bob%20Beatty.pdf

5. "Mexico Frees Slaves," Texas State Historical Association, http://www.tshaonline.org/day-by-day/30416

6. "The Historic Underground Railroad," National Underground Railroad Freedom Center, http://freedomcenter.org/underground-railroad/history/what

7. "Levi Coffin House," Waynet, http://www.waynet.org/levicoffin/

8. Levi Coffin, *Reminiscences of Levi Coffin, the Reputed President of the Underground Railroad* (Cincinnati: Robert Clarke & Co., 1880), p. 112.

9. "The Rankin House," *Midwest Living.* http://www.midwestliving.com/travel/ohio/the-rankin-house/

10. "Rev. John Rankin," National Underground Railroad Freedom Center, http://freedomcenter.org/journey-to-freedom/network/rev-john-rankin

11. Ohio History Central: "John Rankin," http://www.ohiohistorycentral.org/w/John_Rankin

12. *Whispers of Angels: A Story of the Underground Railroad,* "Thomas Garrett," http://www.whispersofangels.com/biographies.html

Chapter 5. Touring the U.G.R.R.

1. Spring Hill Historic Home (private tour), http://www.springhillhistorichome.org/

2. Marilyn Bauer, "Slave Pens Now Hold History," *The Cincinnati Enquirer,* February 8, 2004, http://www.enquirer.com/editions/2004/02/08/slavepen/tem_sunlede08.html

3. Ed Dwight, *International Underground Railroad Memorial,* http://www.eddwight.com/memorial-public-art/international-underground-railroad-memorial-detroit-mi-windsor-canada

4. "Frederick Douglass on Abraham Lincoln: The Writer and Abolitionist Remembers the President in Library of Congress Primary Sources," Library of Congress Blog, http://blogs.loc.gov/teachers/2013/02/frederick-douglass-on-abraham-lincoln-the-writer-and-abolitionist-remembers-the-president-in-library-of-congress-primary-sources/

5. "Frederick Douglass: Freedom In New Bedford," *New Bedford Historical Society,* http://www.umassd.edu/media/umassdartmouth/undergroundrailroad/readings/nb_douglass_2.pdf

6. Sarah Ives, "Did Quilts Hold Codes to the Underground Railroad?" *National Geographic News,* http://news.nationalgeographic.com/news/2004/02/0205_040205_slavequilts.html

Books

Adler, David. *Harriet Tubman and the Underground Railroad.* New York: Holiday House, 2012.

Carson, Mary Kay. *The Underground Railroad for Kids: From Slavery to Freedom with 21 Activities.* Chicago: Chicago Review Press, 2005.

Lassieur, Allison. *The Underground Railroad: An Interactive History Adventure.* Mankato, MN: Capstone Press, 2013.

Tarshis, Lauren. "From Slavery to Freedom." *Storyworks,* February/March 2013, pp. 4–9.

Works Consulted

Bordewich, Fergus M. "Free At Last." *Smithsonian,* December 2004, pp. 64–71.

Brown, Henry Box. *Narrative of the Life of Henry Box Brown, Written by Himself.* Manchester, England: Lee and Glynn, 1851.

Coffin, Levi. *Reminiscences of Levi Coffin: The Reputed President of the Underground Railroad.* Cincinnati: Robert Clarke & Co., 1880.

"The Emergence of Henry 'Box' Brown," *University of North Carolina Free Press.* http://uncpress.unc.edu/pdfs/SampleChapters/9780807831960_ernest_narrative_introsec1.pdf

Faires, Nora. "Across the Border to Freedom: The International Underground Railroad Memorial and the Meanings of Migration." *Journal of American Ethnic History,* Winter 2013, pp. 38–67.

Frost, Karolyn Smardz. "From Detroit to the Promised Land." *American History,* April 2007, pp. 40–45.

McCarty, Laura P. "Bound for Freedom." *National Parks,* November/December 1991, pp. 32–36.

"Ohio's Underground Railroad to Freedom." *Ohio State Parks Magazine,* Spring/Summer 1996. http://www.dnr.state.oh.us/parks/magazinehome/magazine/sprsum96/undergrr/tabid/299/default.aspx

"Retracing the Route to Freedom." *National Parks,* November/December 1996, pp. 40–43.

Rosen, Marty. "Gateway to Freedom." *Louisville Magazine,* October 2012, pp. 42–45.

Still, William. *Still's Underground Railroad Records, Revised Edition.* Philadelphia: William Still, Publisher, 1886.

Underground Railroad Information Station, Ohio Historical Society, http://ww2.ohiohistory.org/undergroundrr/

Wyels, Joyce Gregory. "Harriet Tubman: Underground Railroad Byway." *American Road,* Autumn 2013, pp. 70–75.

On the Internet

History: "The Underground Railroad"
http://www.history.com/topics/underground-railroad

"Myths of the Underground Railroad"
http://teacher.scholastic.com/activities/bhistory/underground_railroad/myths.htm

National Geographic Education: "The Underground Railroad"
http://education.nationalgeographic.com/education/multimedia/interactive/the-underground-railroad/?ar_a=1

National Park Service: "Aboard the Underground Railroad"
http://www.cr.nps.gov/Nr/travel/underground/

National Park Service: "Network to Freedom"
http://www.nps.gov/subjects/ugrr/about_ntf/index.htm

National Underground Railroad Freedom Center: "The Underground Railroad"
http://freedomcenter.org/underground-railroad-0

PBS—People and Events: "The Underground Railroad"
http://www.pbs.org/wgbh/aia/part4/4p2944.html

Underground Railroad Information Station, Ohio Historical Society, http://ww2.ohiohistory.org/undergroundrr/

"The Underground Railroad: Escape from Slavery"
http://teacher.scholastic.com/activities/bhistory/underground_railroad/

abolitionist (ab-uh-LIH-shuh-nist)—A person who believed that slavery was wrong and worked to abolish, or end, it.

clergy (KLUR-jee)—An official in a church or other religious institution.

concentration camp (kon-sun-TRAY-shun KAMP)—A camp where people such as political prisoners or refugees are held.

discrimination (deh-skrih-mih-NAY-shun)—The treating of some people better than other people for unfair reasons.

endorse (en-DORS)—To recommend.

exodus (EK-soh-dus)—Flight by a large group of people.

expedient (ek-SPEE-dee-ent)—Efficient, quick.

fugitive (FYOO-jih-tiv)—A person who is running away illegally.

North Star, Big Dipper, and Small Dipper—Objects in the sky that runaway slaves would use to guide themselves northward to freedom.

outmoded (owt-MOH-ded)—No longer suitable or acceptable.

perpetuate (per-PET-choo-ayt)—To cause [something] to continue.

reenactment (ree-en-AKT-ment)—A play or other performance that depicts actual events.

sovereignty (SAH-vrun-tee)—Power to rule.

stipulation (stih-pyoo-LAY-shun)—A condition or requirement included in a formal agreement.

sympathetic (sim-pah-THEH-tik)—Feeling the same way as someone else.

U.G.R.R.—An abbreviation for the Underground Railroad that has been used since the mid-1800s.